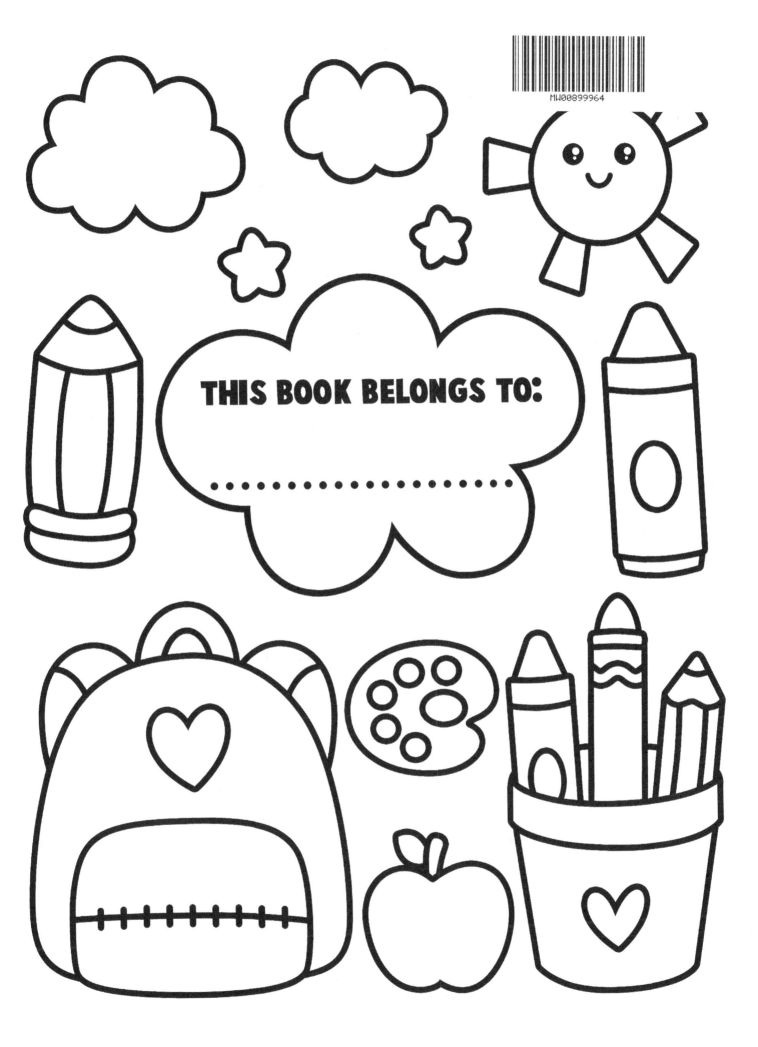

THIS BOOK BELONGS TO:

Thank you!

Thank you so much for purchasing this coloring book!
I hope you absolutely loved it! Be sur to follow
us on Amazon to get updates on new books!

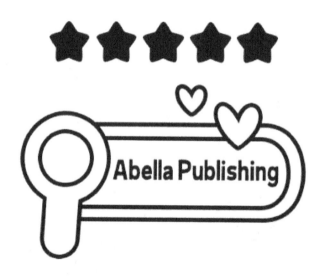

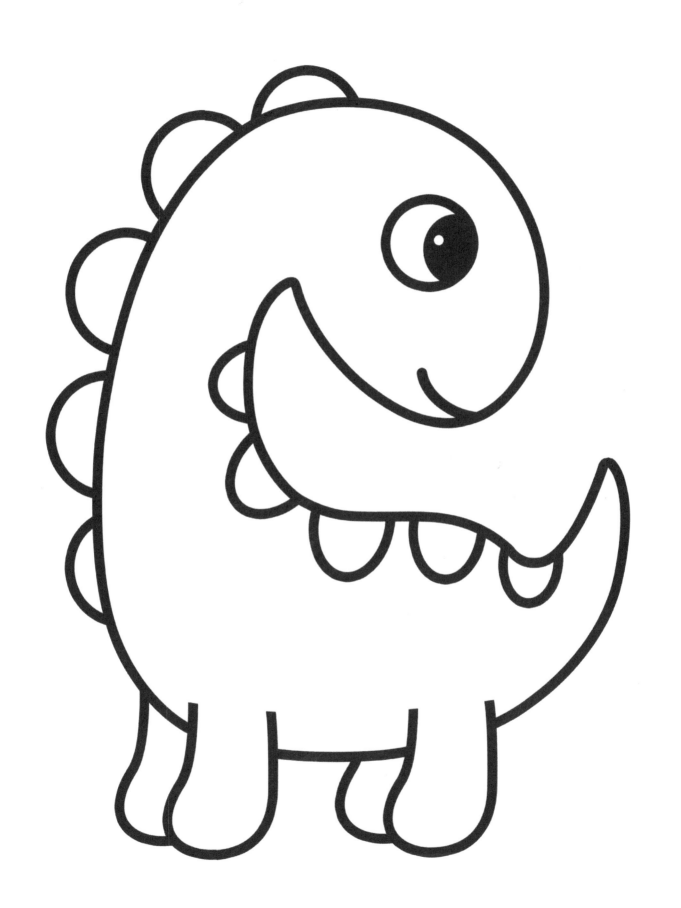

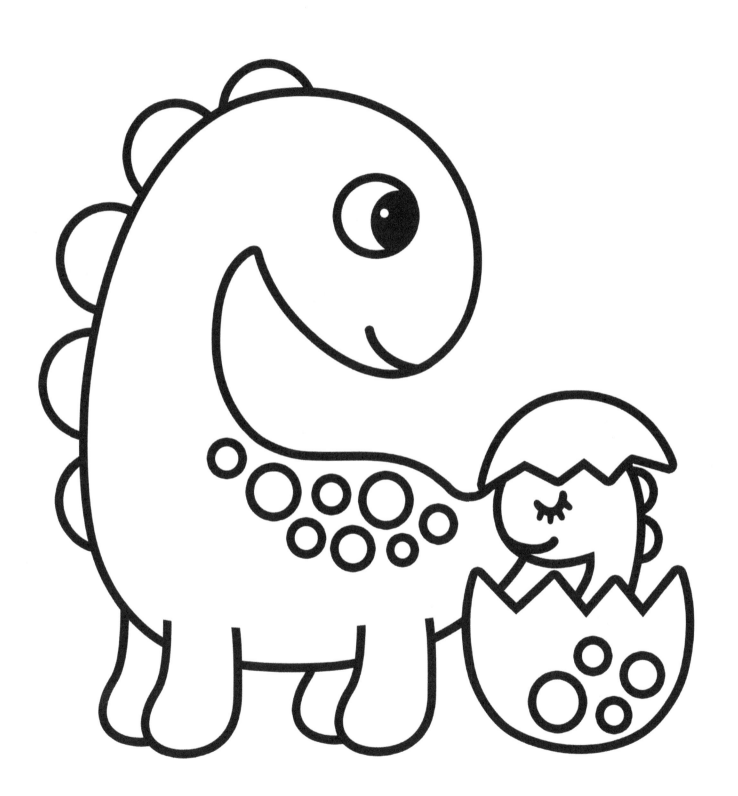

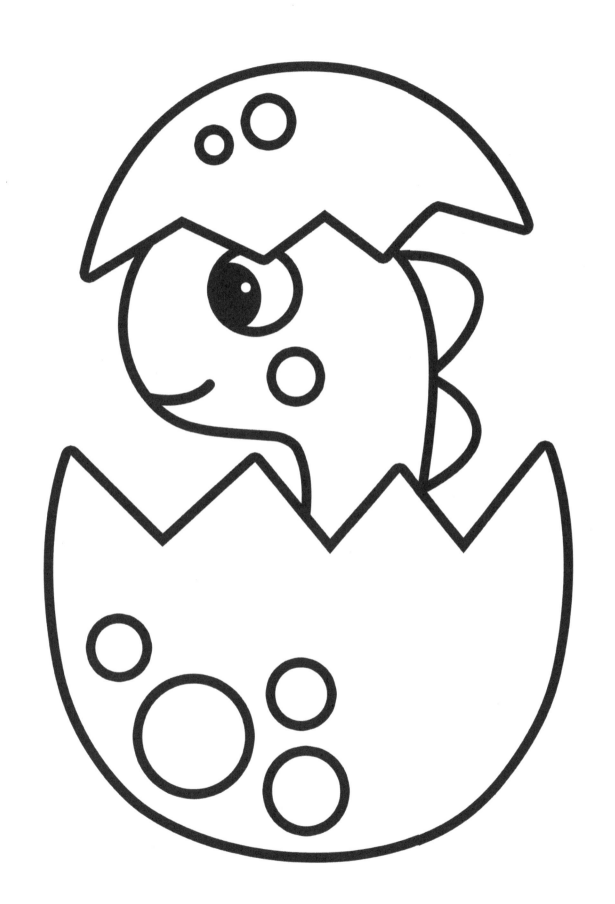

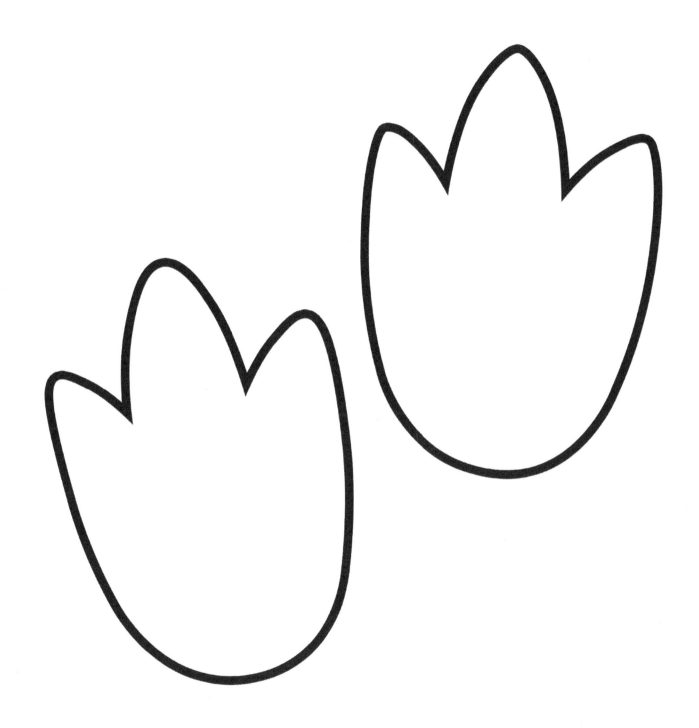

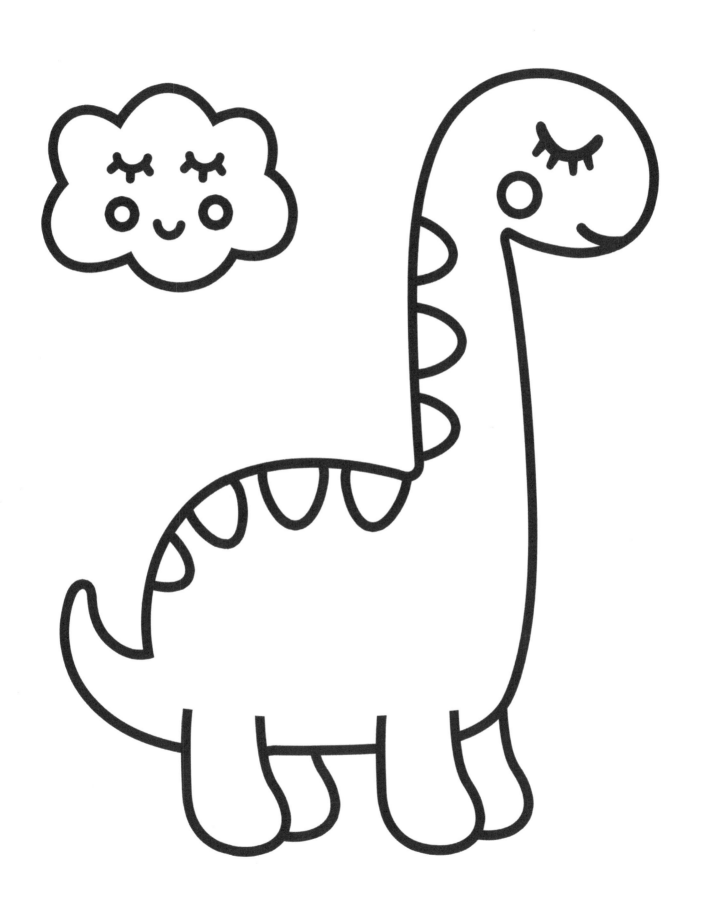

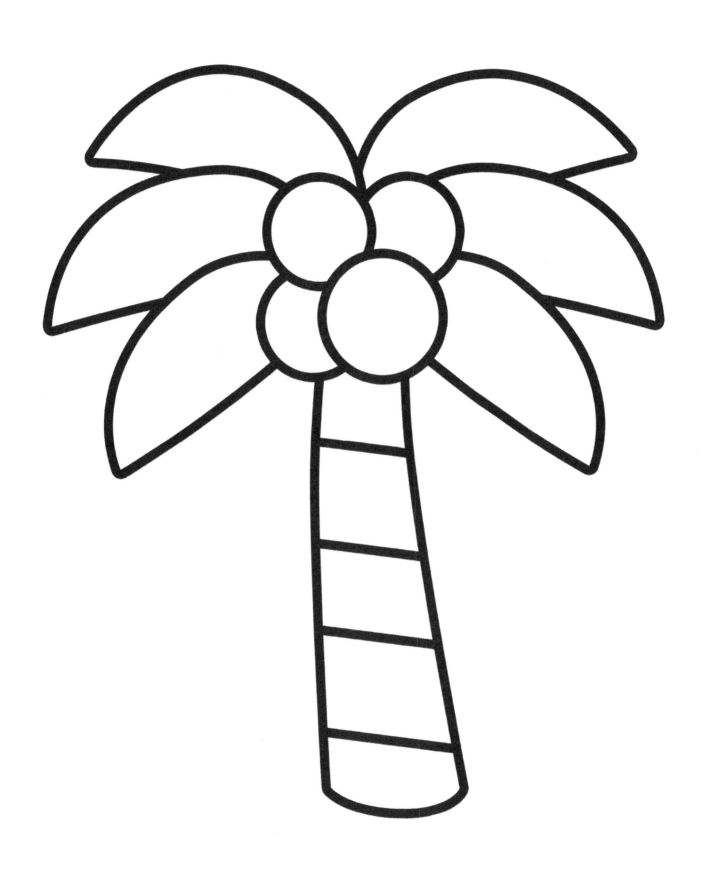

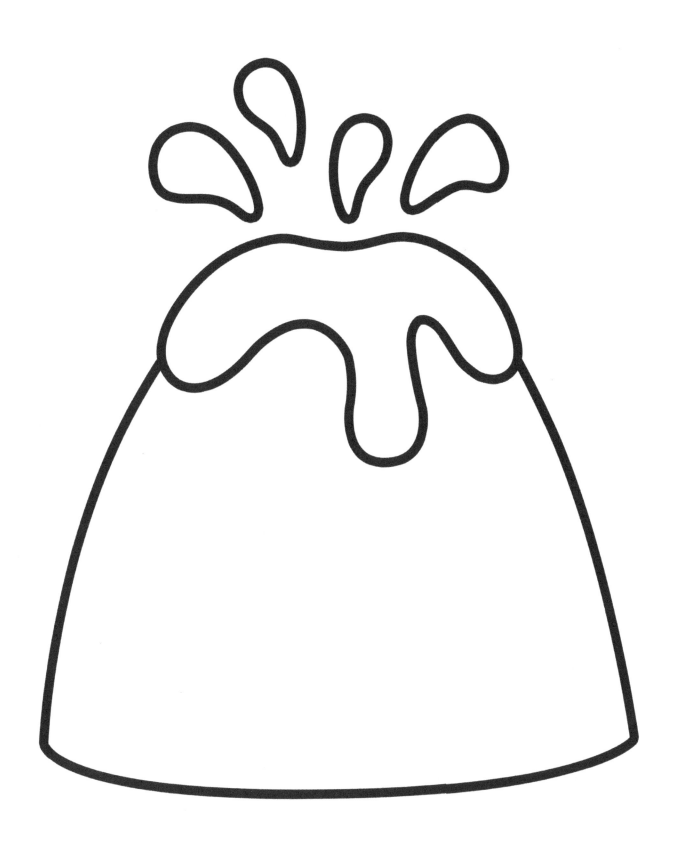

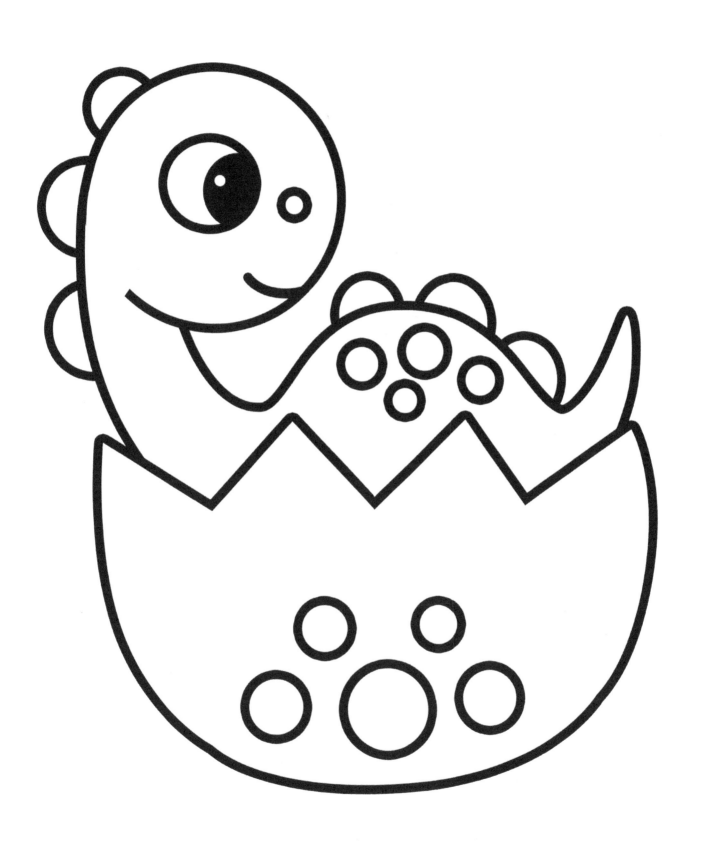

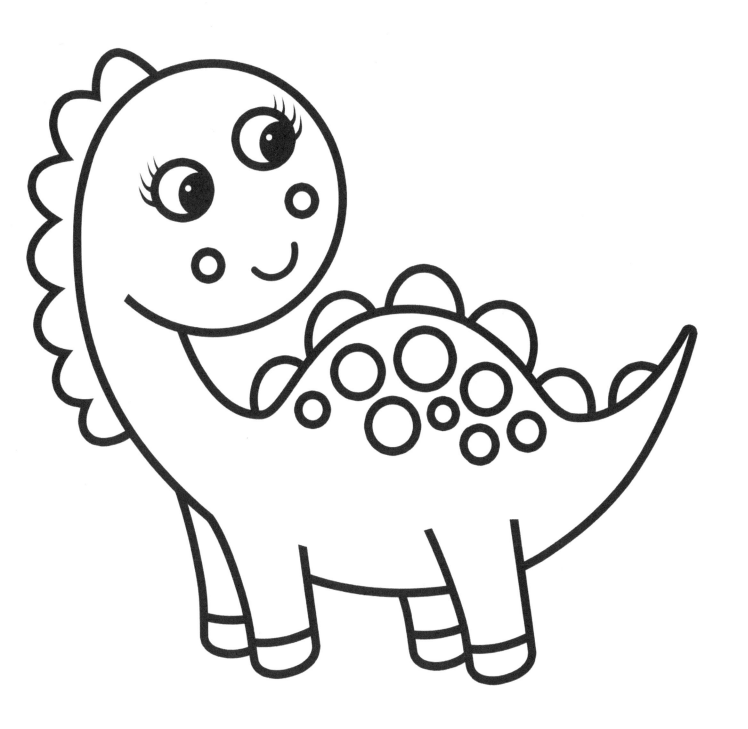

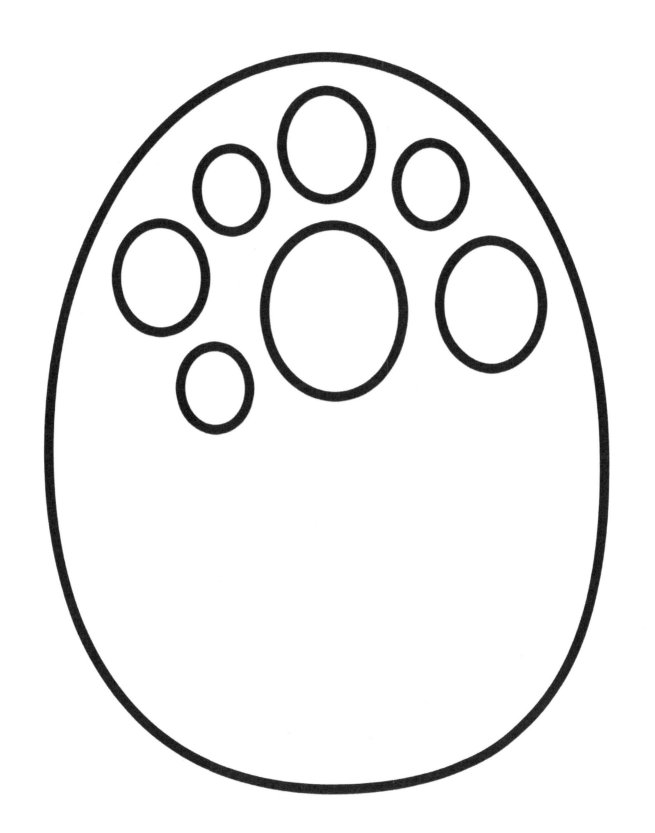

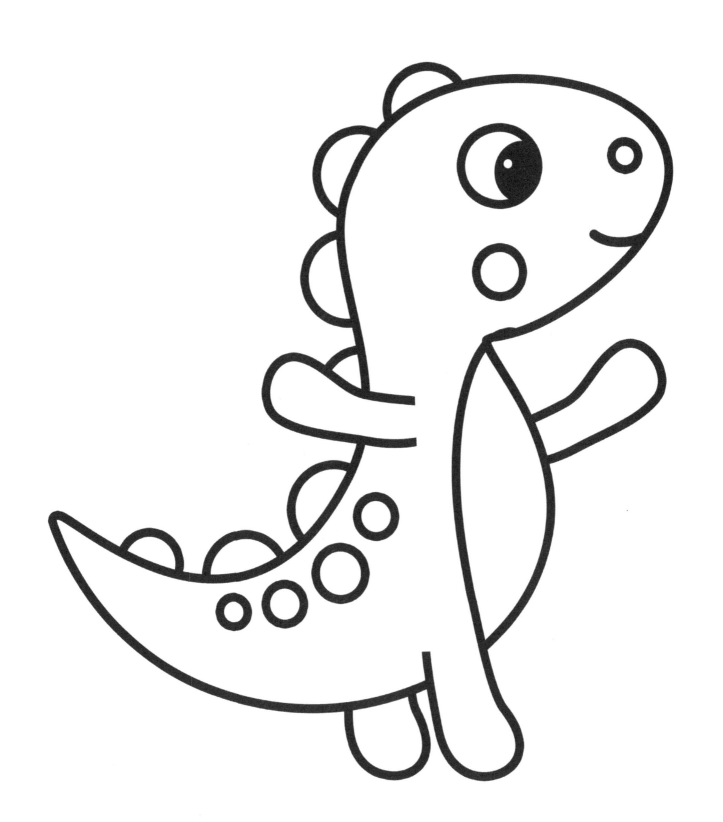

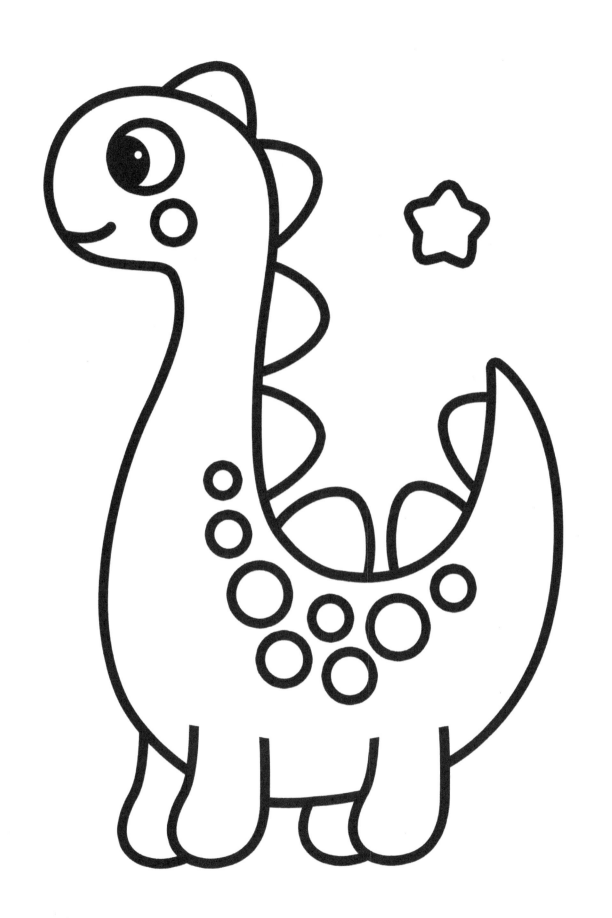

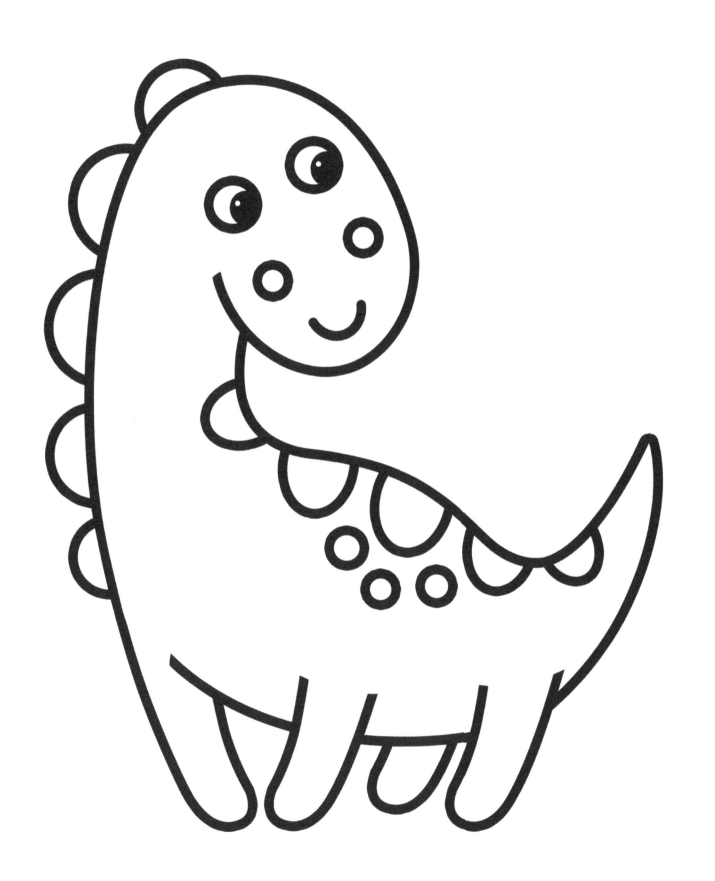

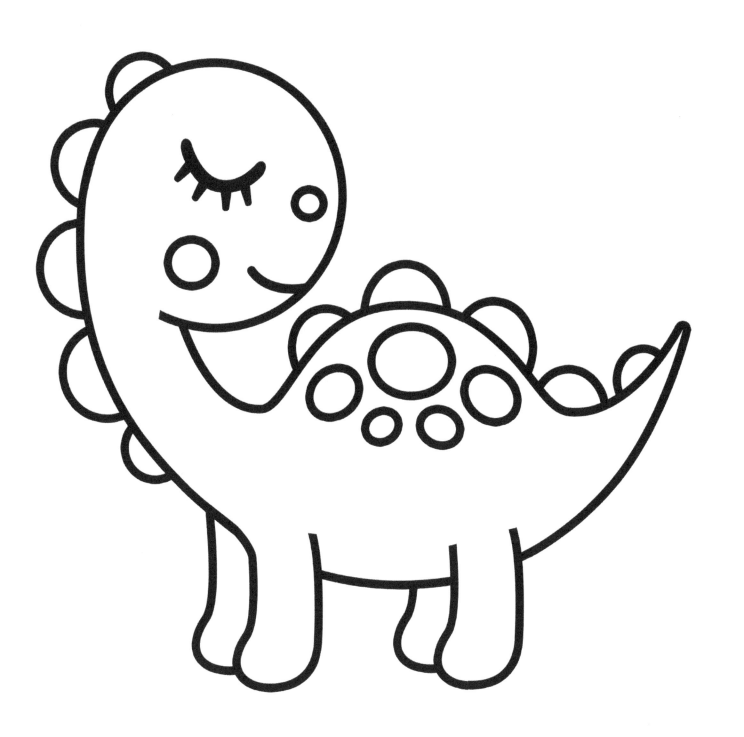

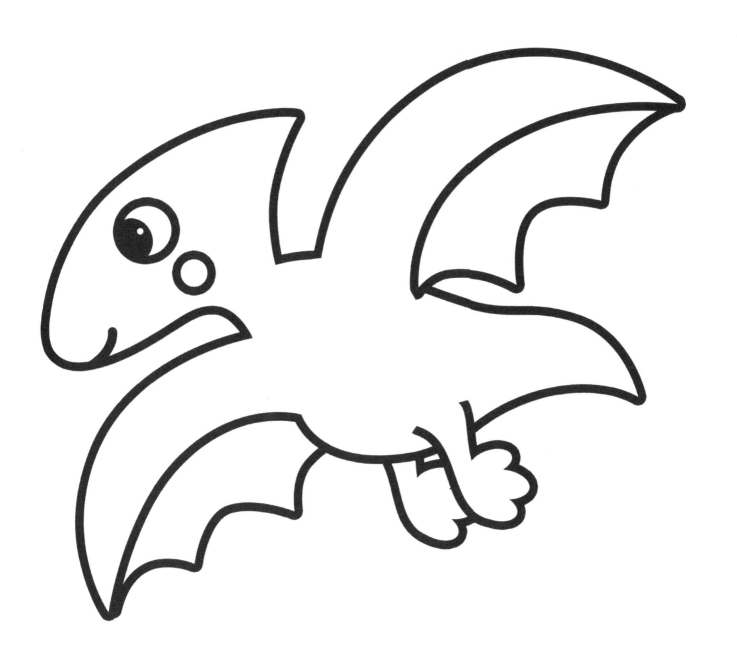

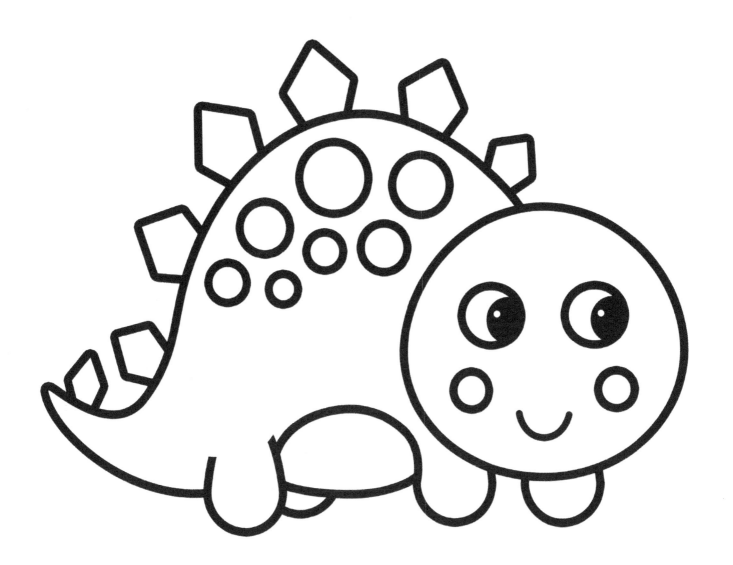

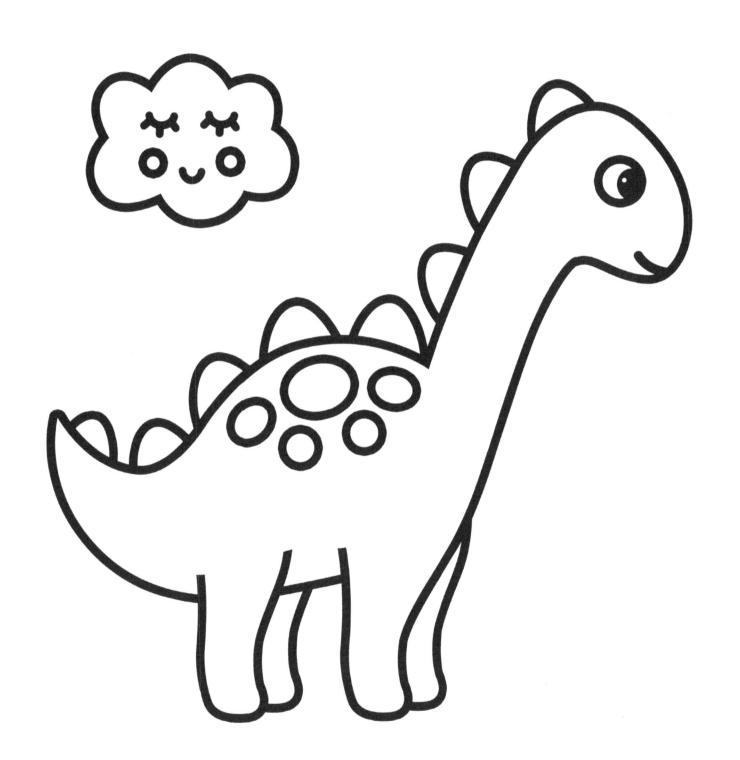

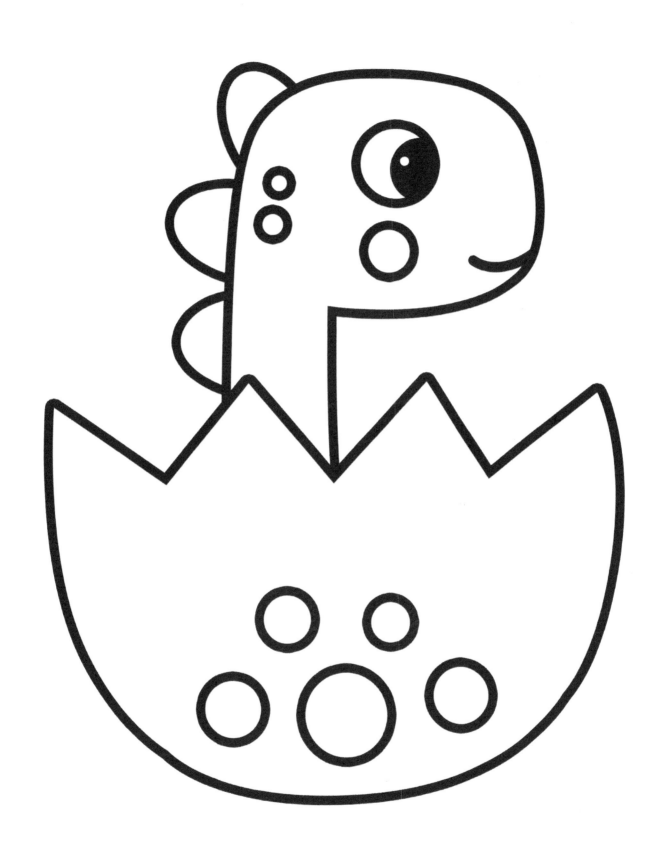

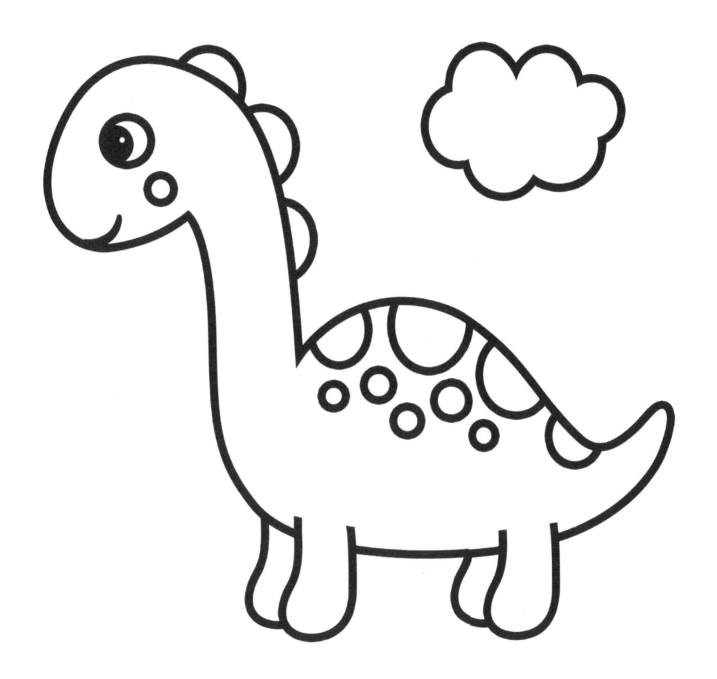

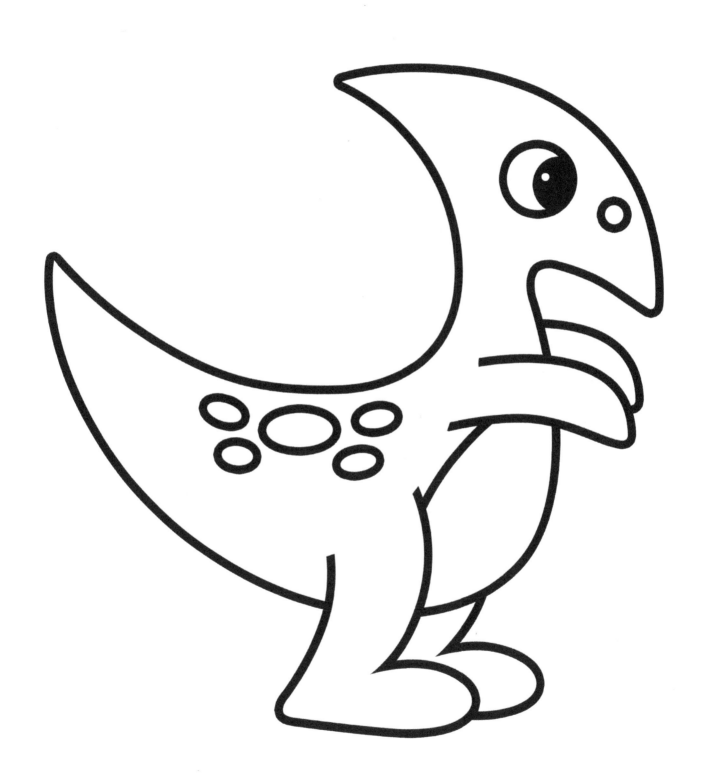

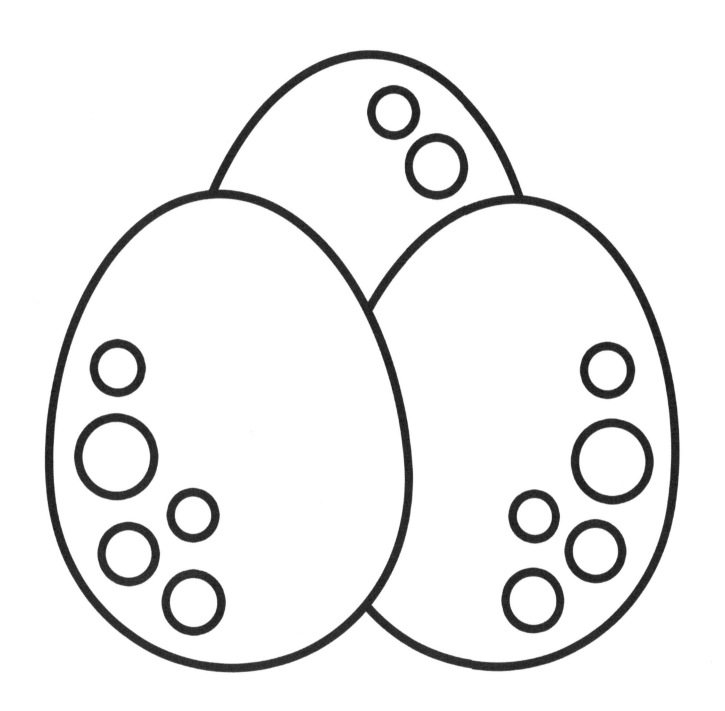

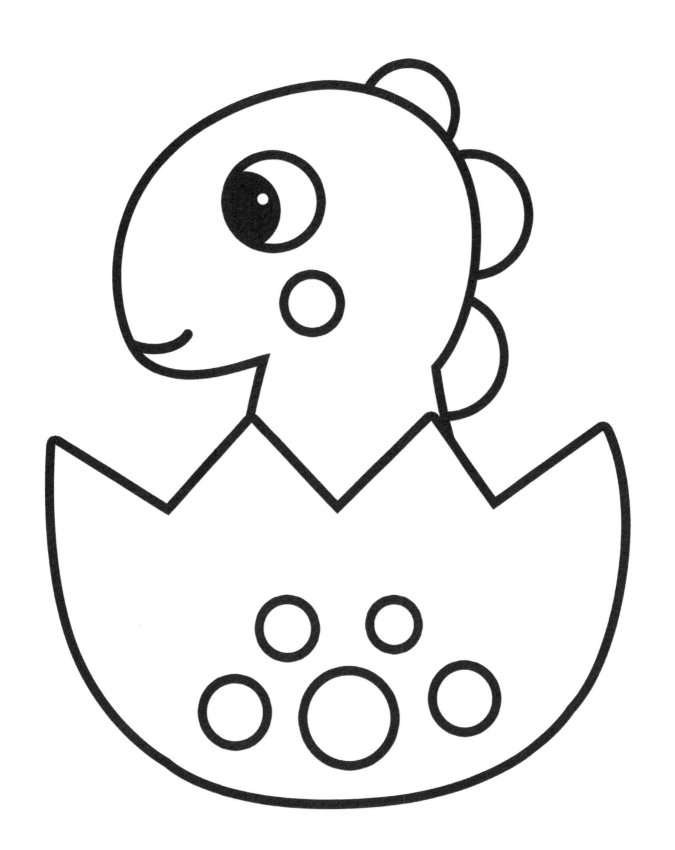

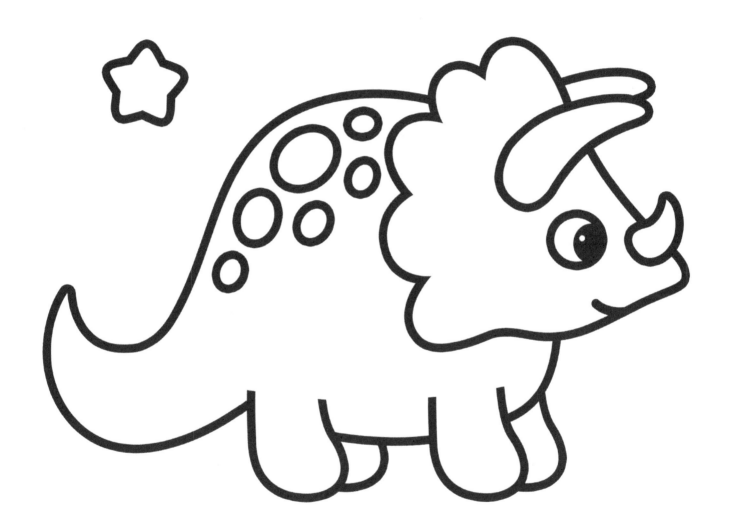

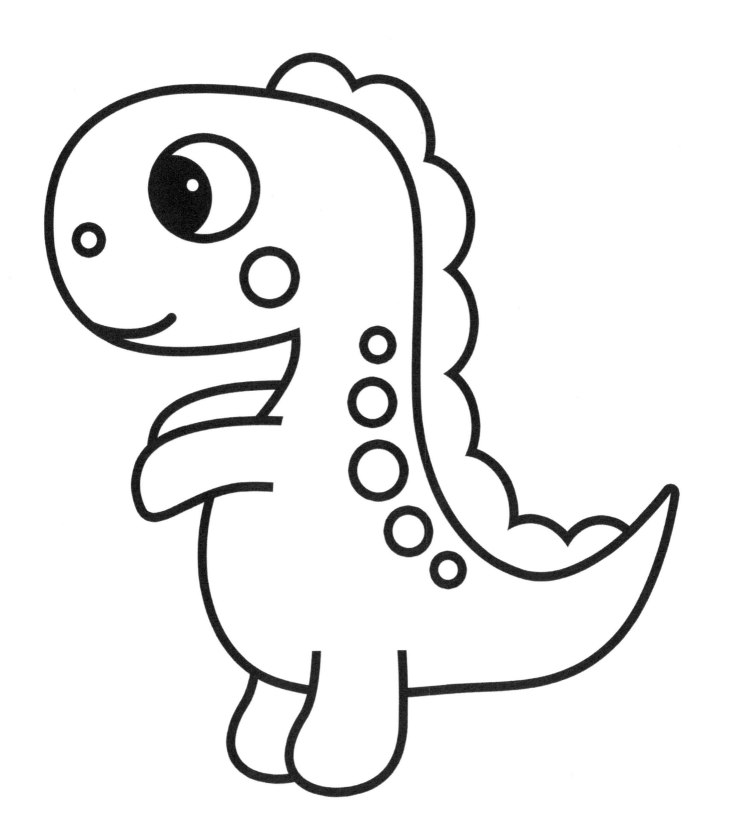

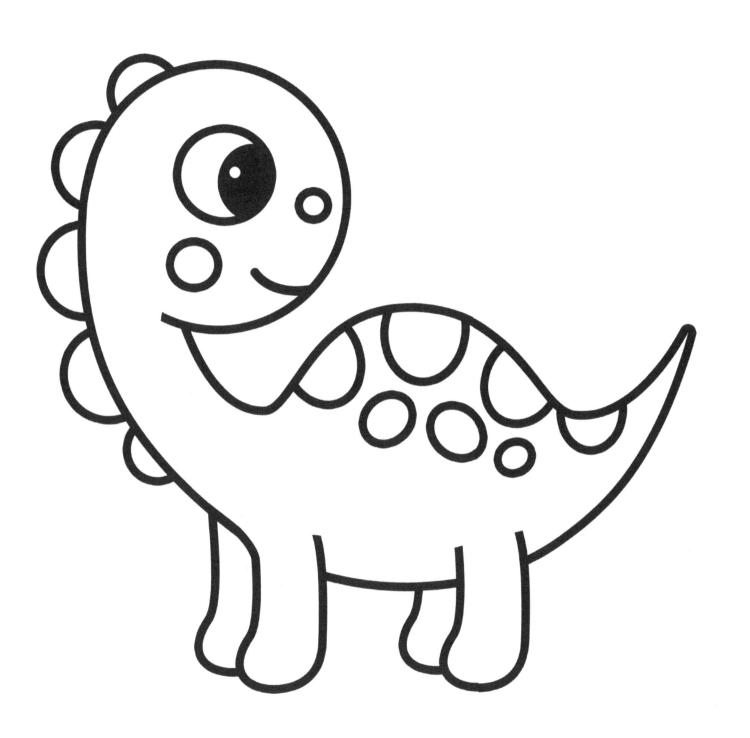

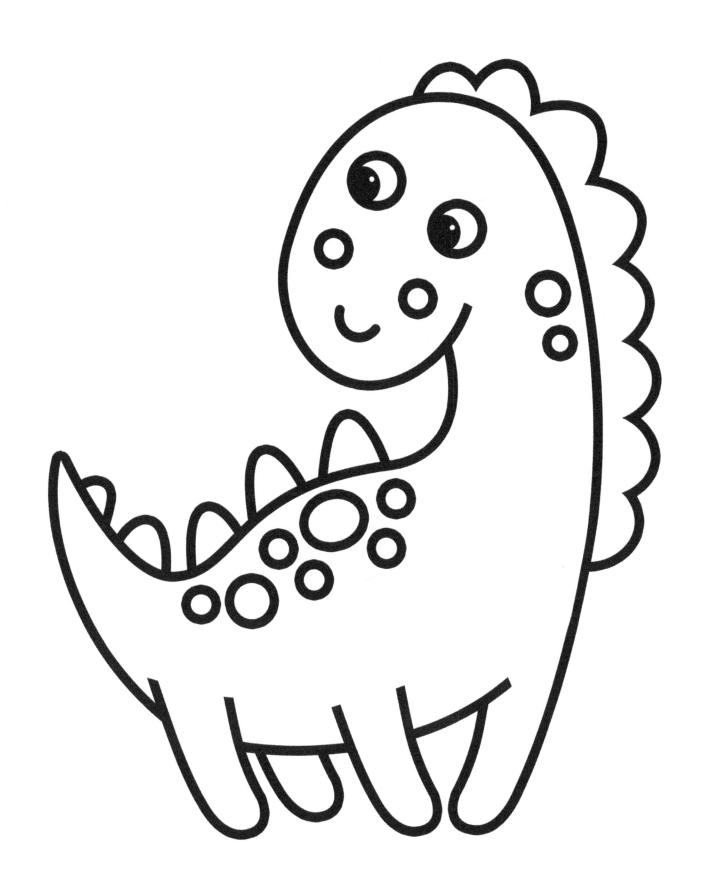

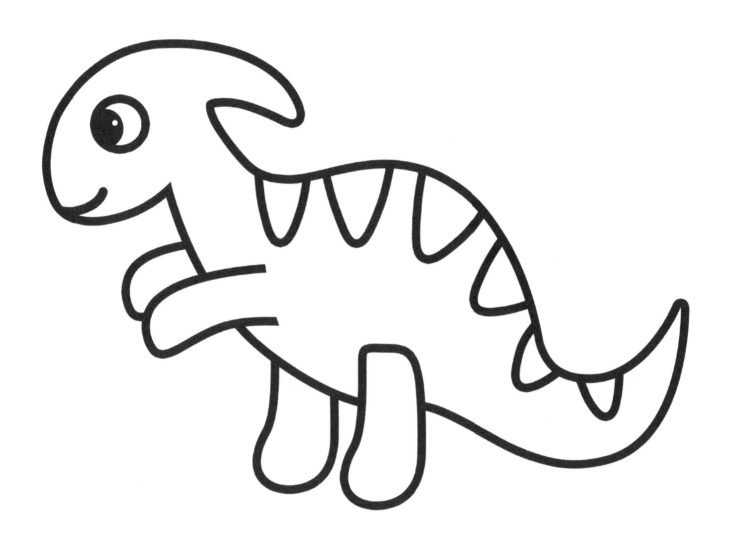

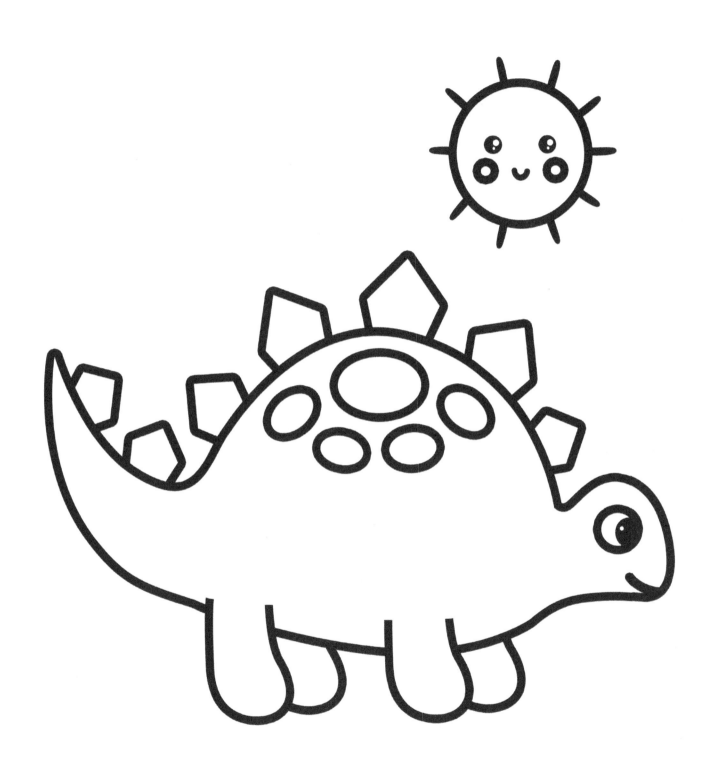

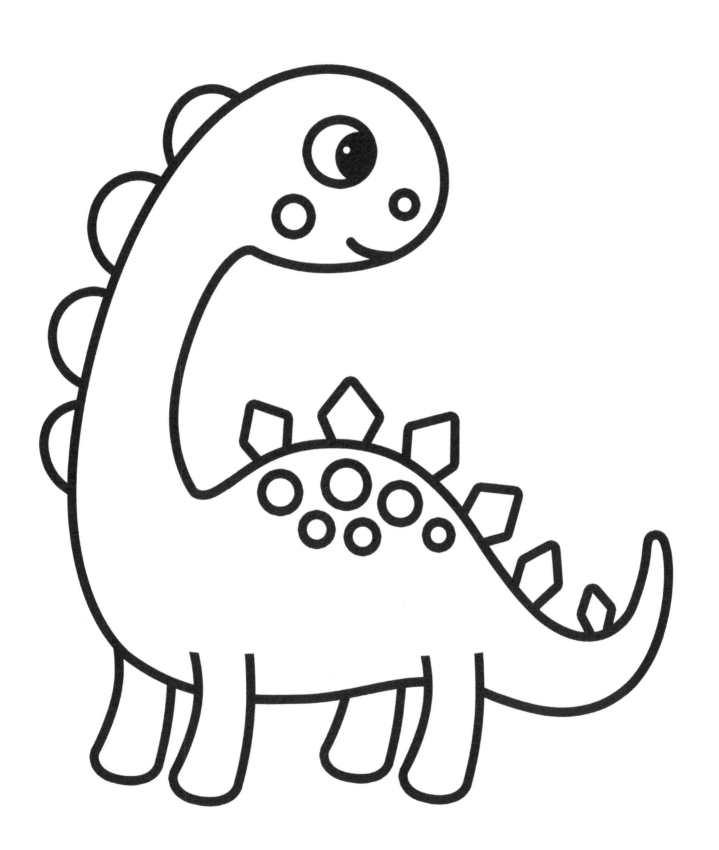

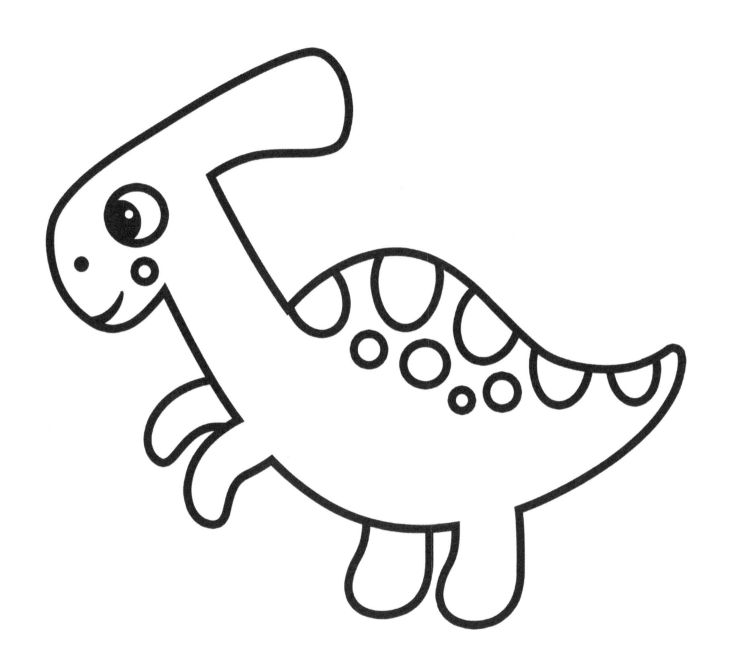

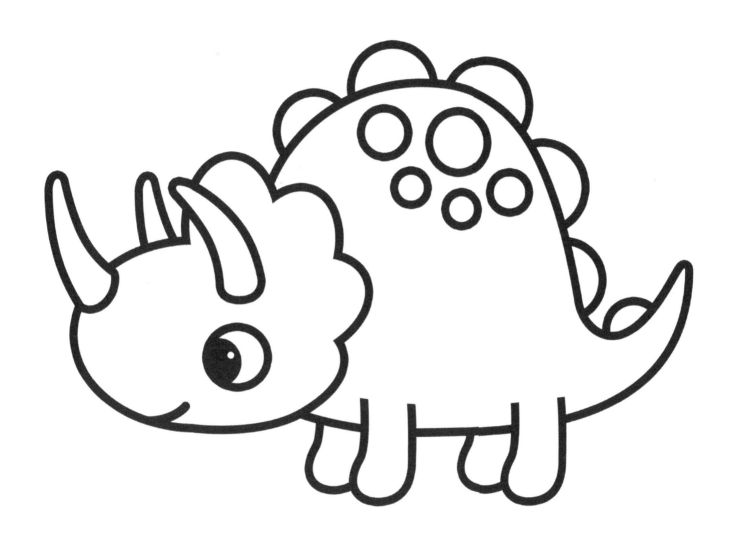

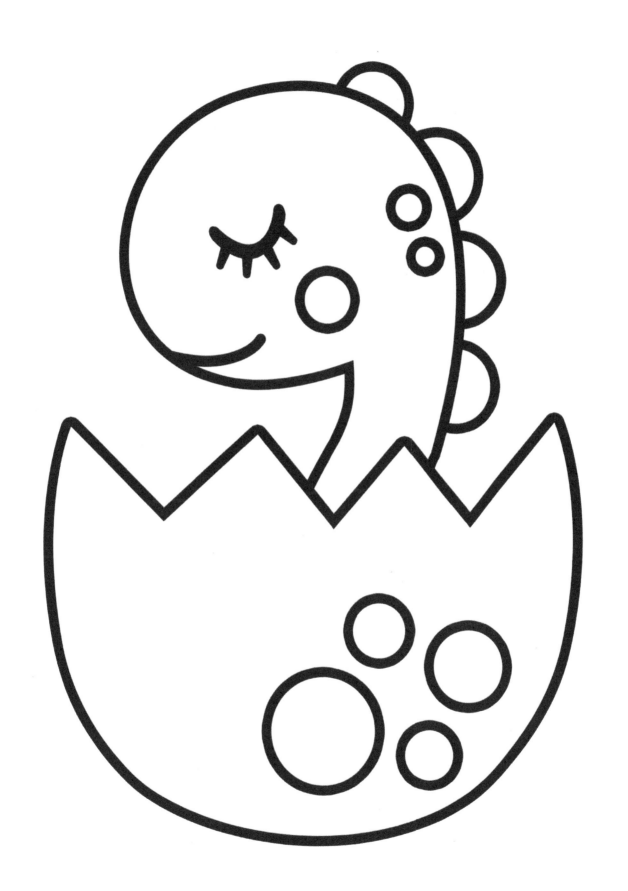

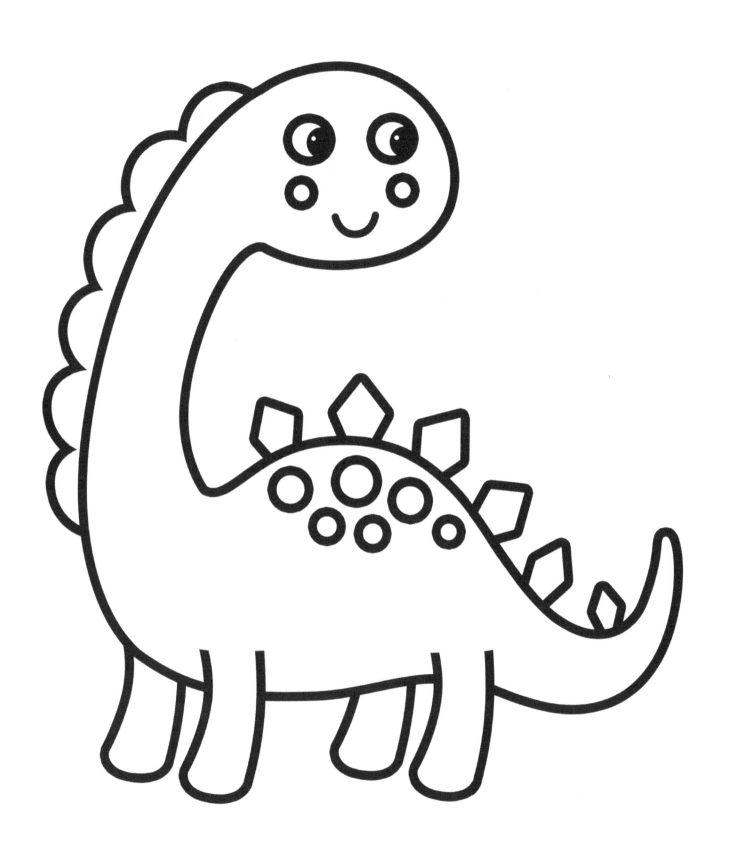

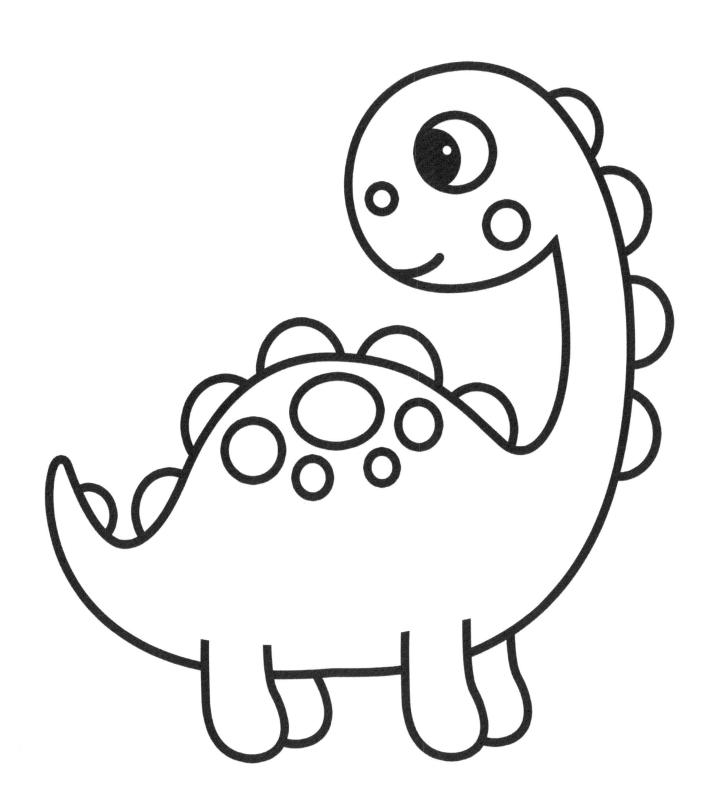

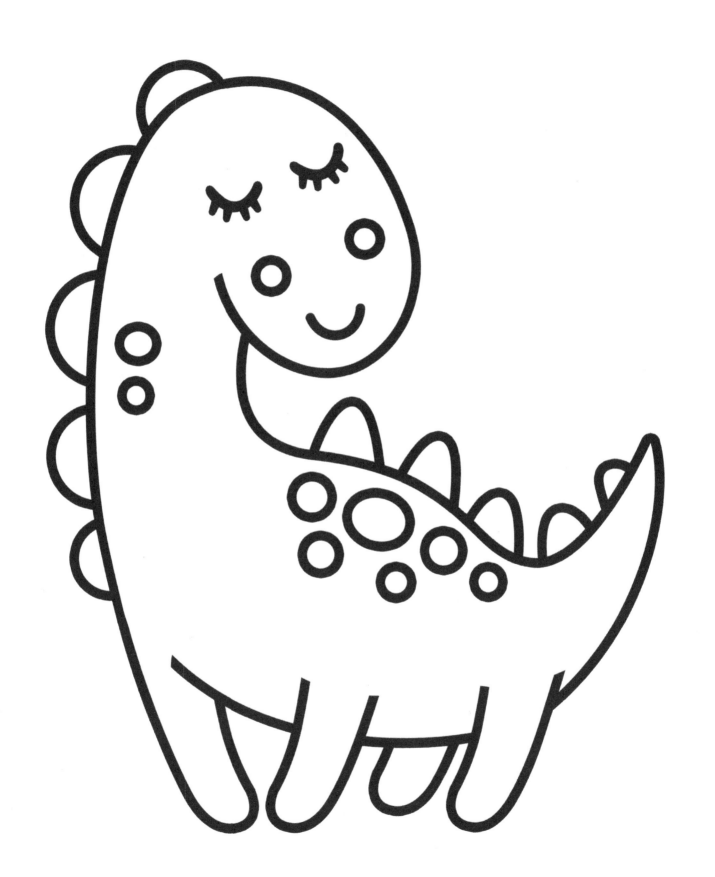

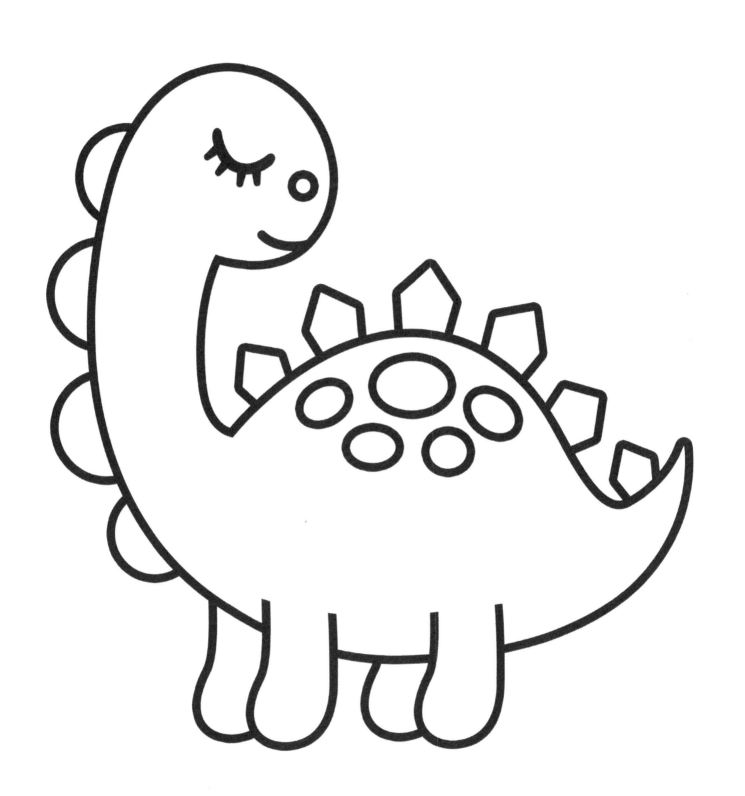

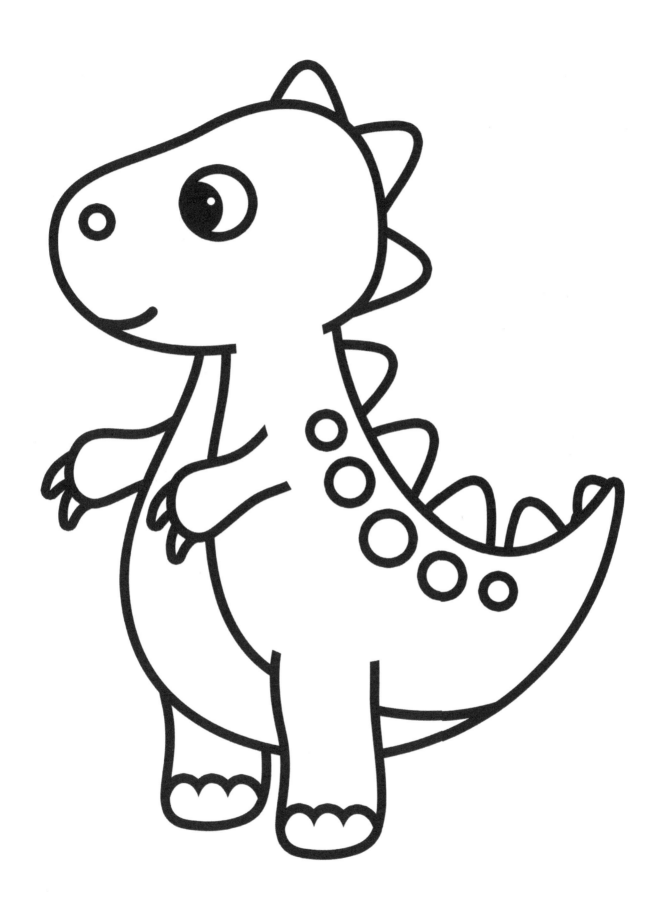

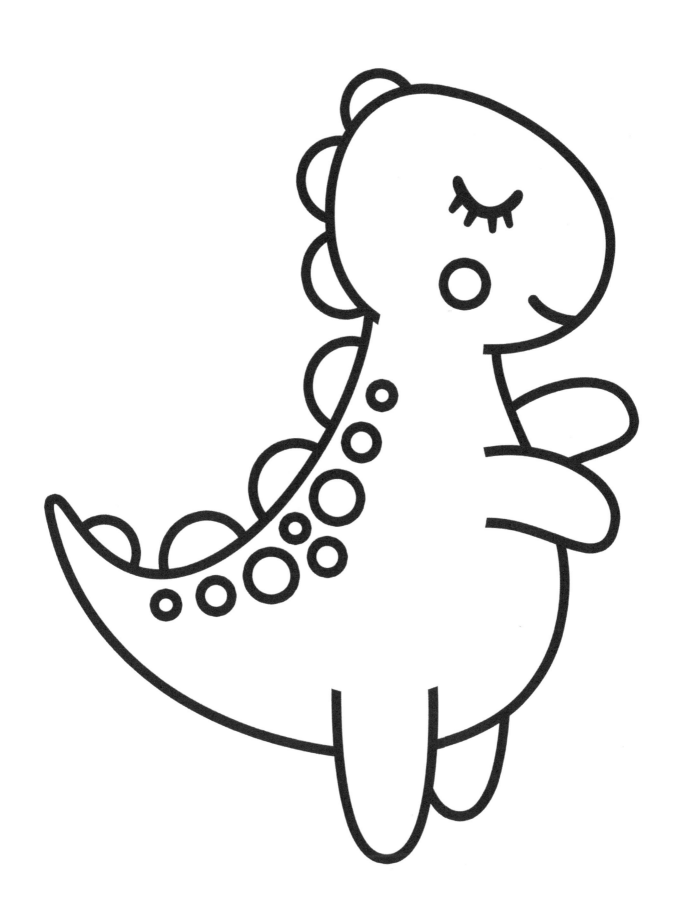

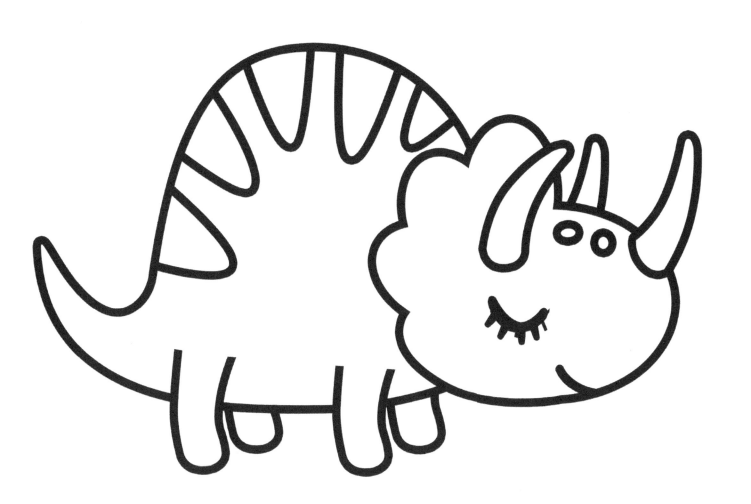

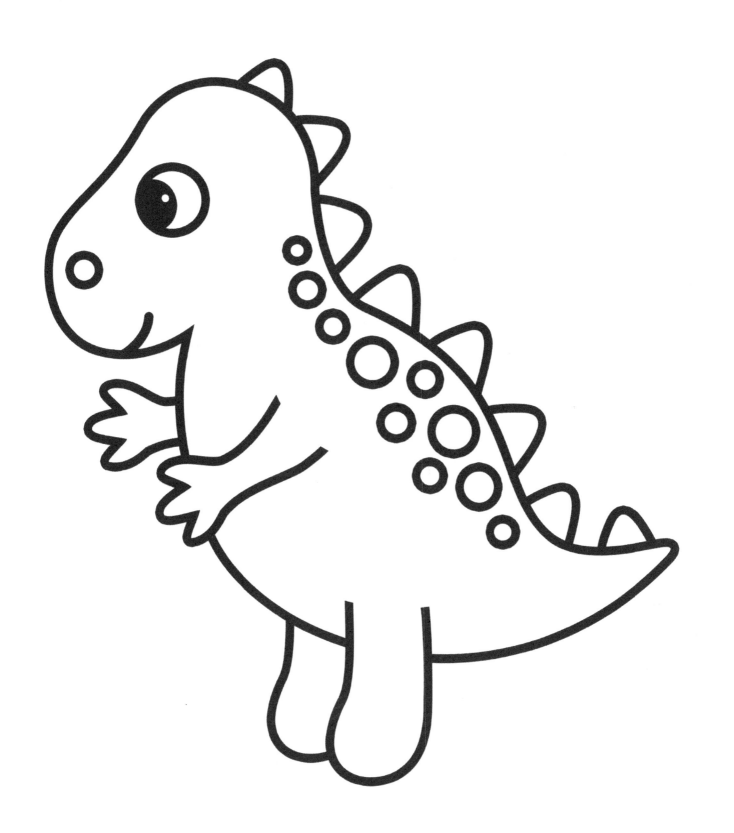

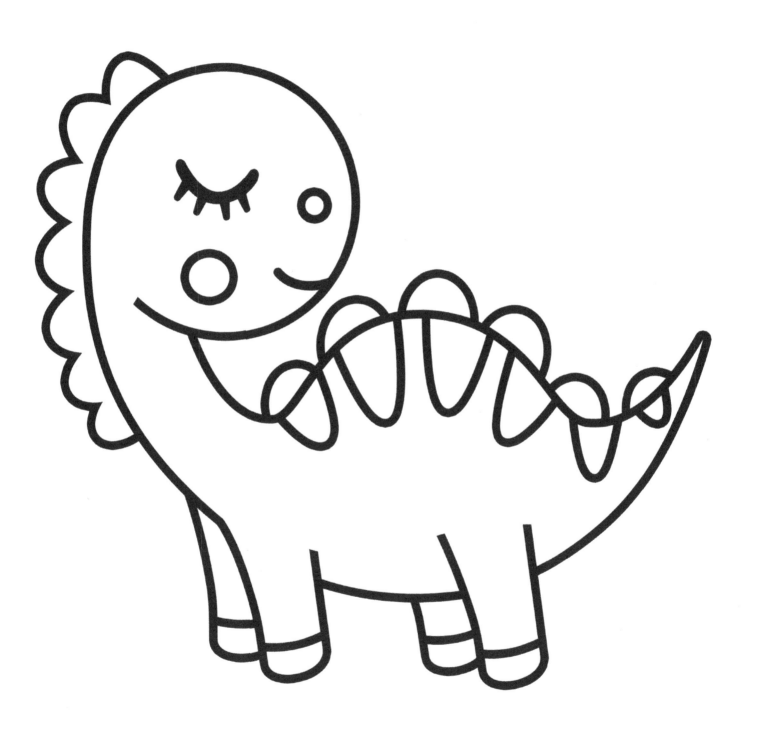

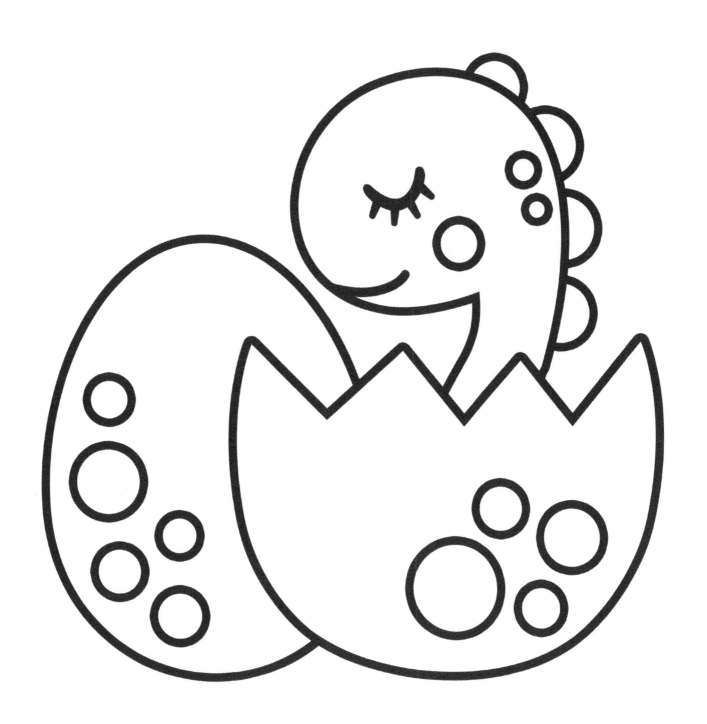

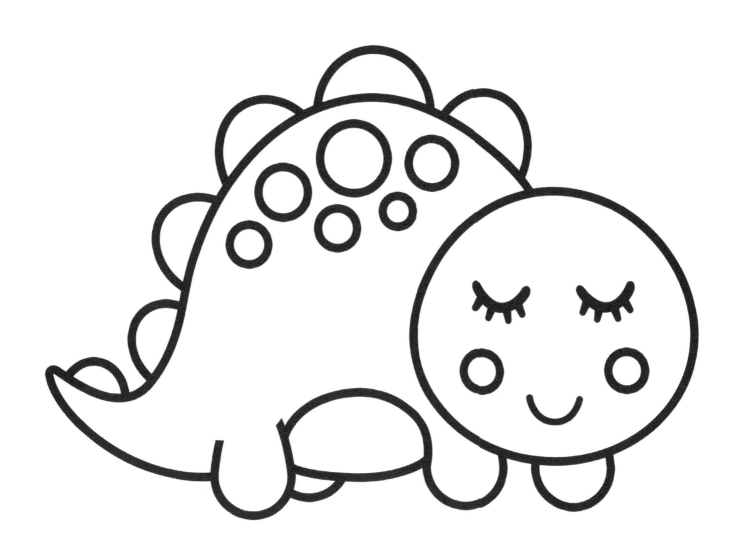

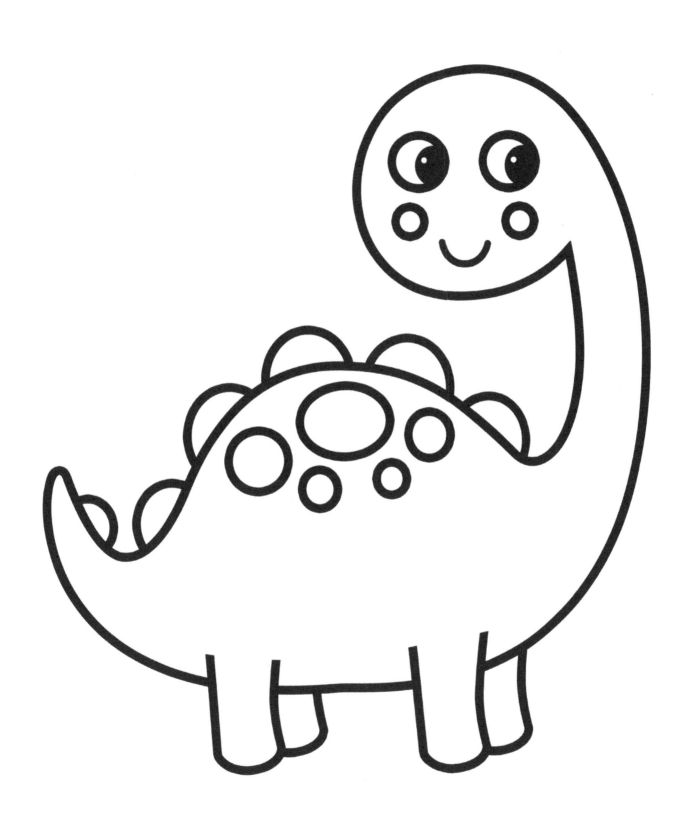

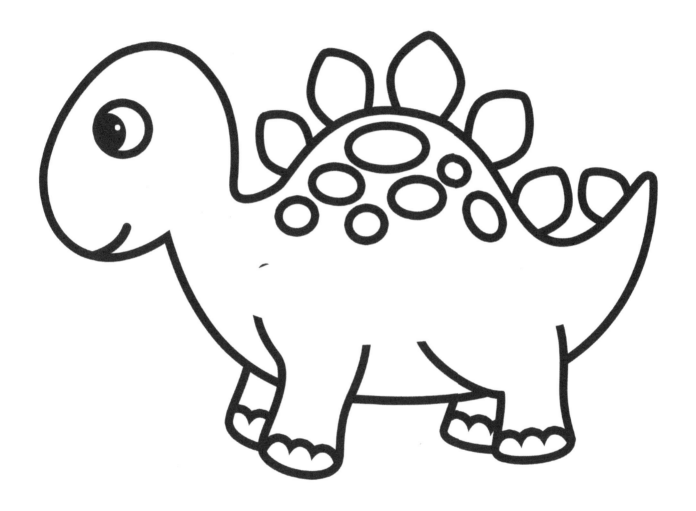

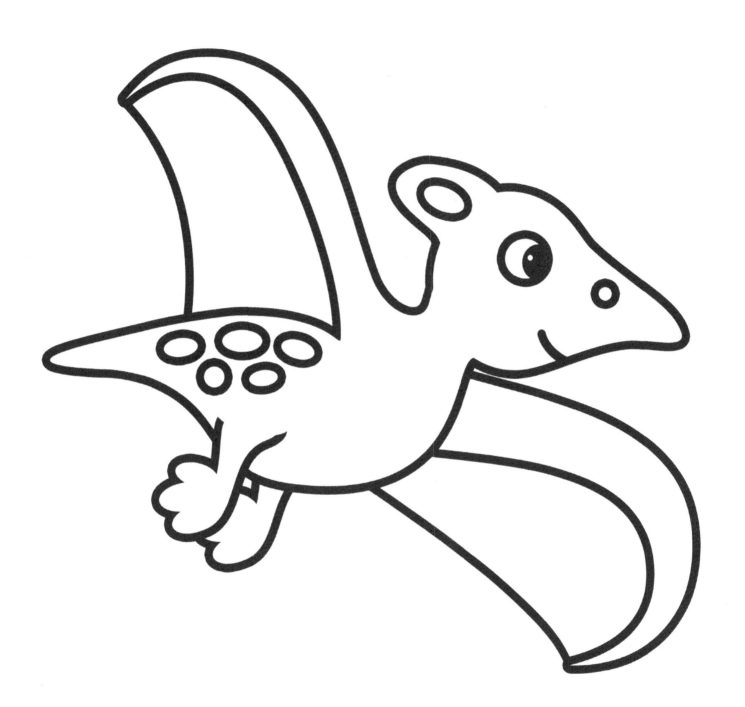

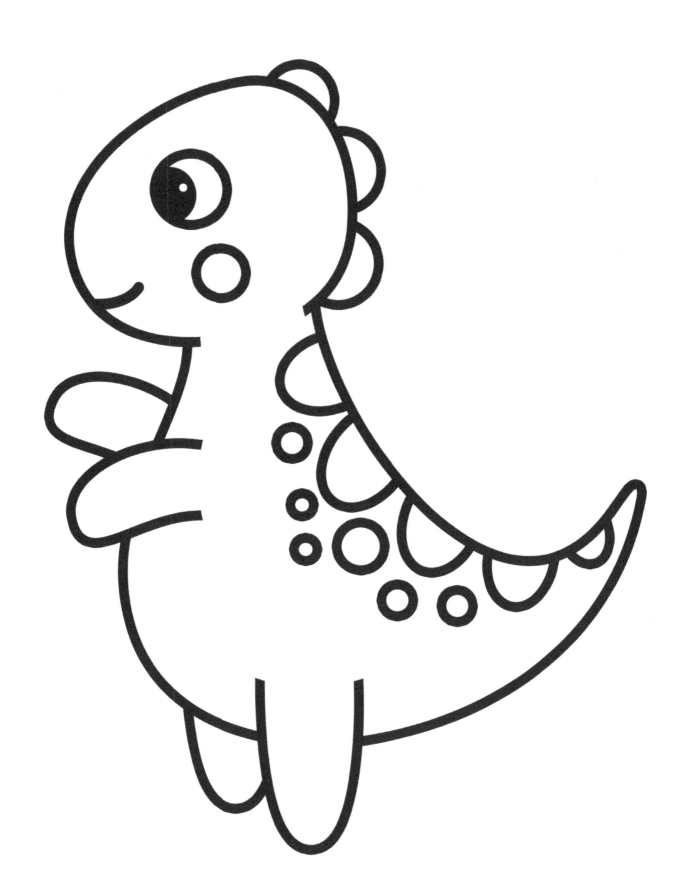

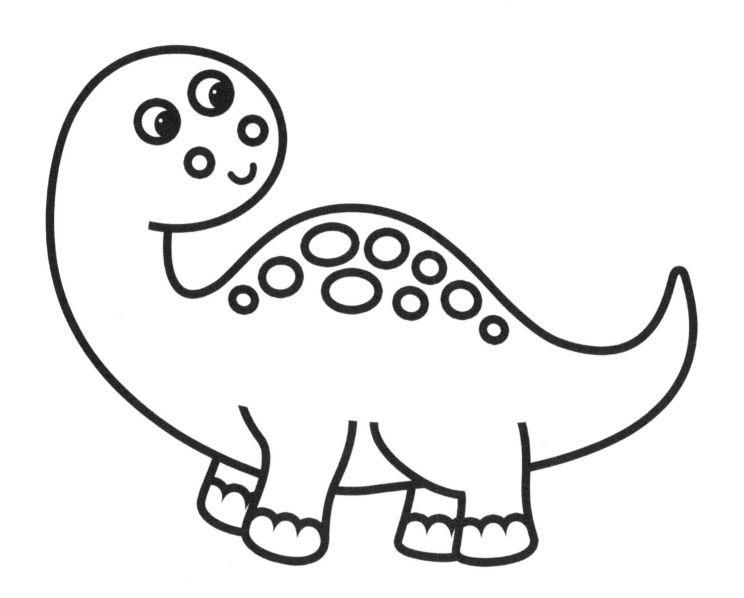

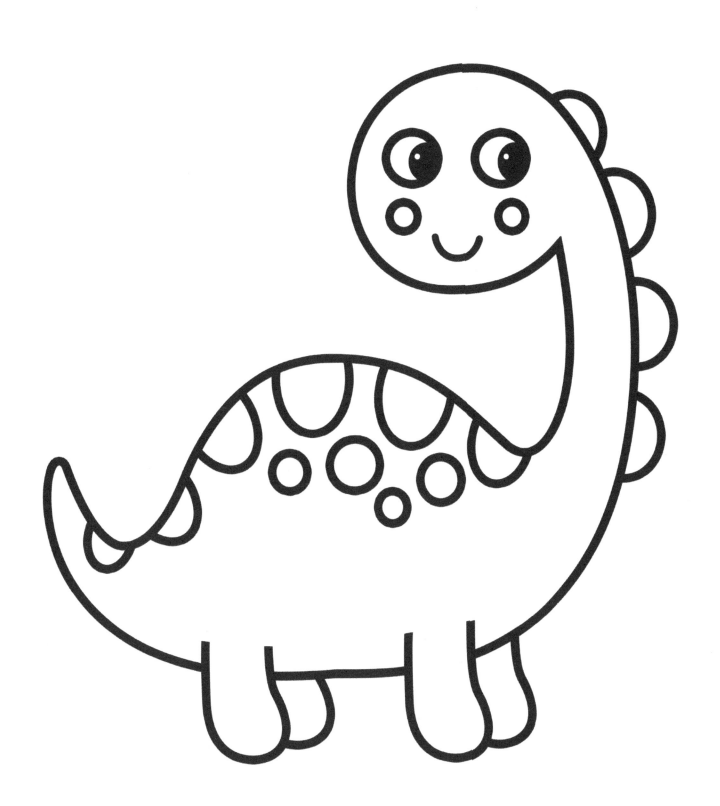

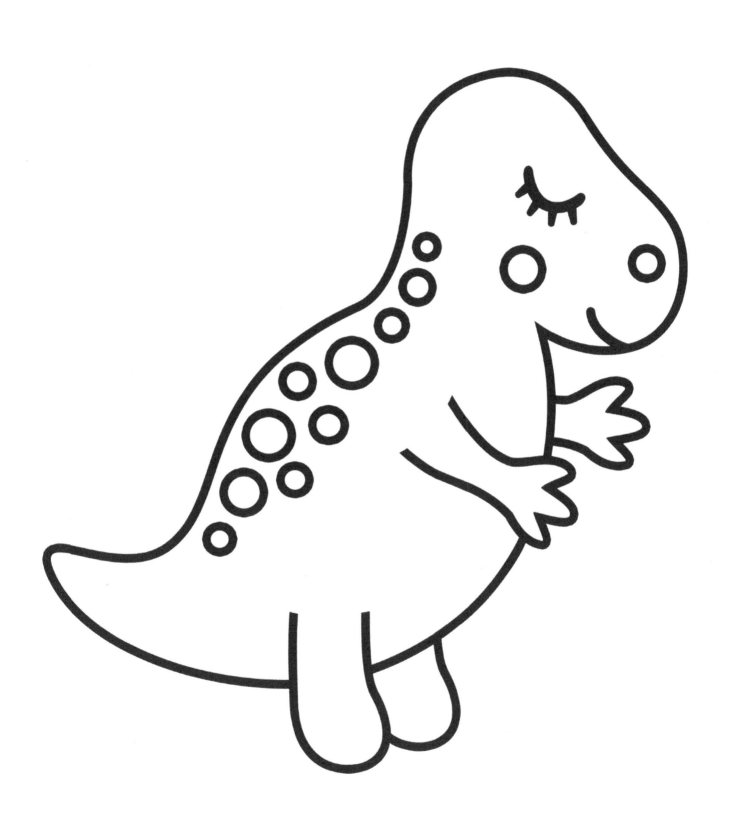

Made in the USA
Columbia, SC
16 December 2024

49309089R00057